MW01064486

The Bumpy Road
To
Enlightenment

Thoughts Collected Along The Path

The Bumpy Road
To
Enlightenment
Thoughts Collected Along The Path

Blessings & Peace

Lori Cardona

Aglob Publishing

Aglob Publishing
Hallandale Beach, Florida

Tel: 954-456-1476
E-Mail: info@aglobpublishing.com
www.aglobpublishing.com

Copyright © 2003 by Lori Cardona

All rights reserved. No part of this book may be reproduced or transmitted in
any form or by any means, electronic or mechanical, including photocopying,
recording or by any information storage and retrieval system without written
permission from the copyright owner and the publisher, except for the inclusion
of brief quotations in a review.

Library of Congress Cataloging-in-Publication Data

Cardona, Lori.
  The bumpy road to enlightenment : thoughts collected along the path /
Lori Cardona.
     p. cm.
  ISBN 0-9708560-3-2
  1. Cardona, Lori. 2. Spiritual biography--United States. I. Title.

  BL73.C345A3 2003
  291.4'092--dc21

                                                              2003007771

Printed in the United States of America

5 4 3 2 1

Dedication

To my loving friends,
both in flesh and in spirit,
who walk beside me along this path.
And, who always help me over the bumps.

Acknowledgements

I often tell people that I've been writing a book, in my head, for the past 25 years. The words have been in there, on dusty shelves, waiting for me to put them down on paper. So now that I've finally found a way, I need to thank all the kind and caring souls who encouraged me, believed in me, supported me, or bought me pens and journals and books. While too many to list, I bow in love and gratitude, to each and every one.

Thanks to She Magazine and the Interfaith Council For Freedom Of Worship for previously publishing some of what you see here.

Thanks to The New Seminary for the education and ordination that has changed my life from ego-driven to God-centered.

Thanks to the bumps encountered along my spiritual path. They opened my eyes and my heart. They strengthened me and they softened me. They've made me a better person.

Most importantly, my deep unwavering gratitude to the ever lasting, awe-inspiring, miraculous source of all that is life and love.

About The Author:

Reverend Lori Cardona is an Interfaith Minister, Educator, Consultant, Writer. With over 25 years experience in the field of Human Services, she holds a Masters Degree in Counseling from the University of North Carolina, and a Doctorate in Divinity from The American Institute of Holistic Theology. She was ordained by The New Seminary, NYC and Independent Unity, Ft. Lauderdale, FL. She currently resides in Miami, Florida while serving as a Hospice Chaplain, Senior Minister Of Interfaith Alliance Ministries, and a therapist in private practice.

Contents

Introduction

There's a story told about the bumpy road to enlightenment that has to do with a Midwestern potato farmer by the name of Frank. Frank and his fellow potato farmers spent a lot of time tending to their crop. Seasons came and seasons went, with tender care applied to growing, nurturing, and choosing the potatoes that were to be taken to town for market sales. One of the most time-consuming and final potato-preparation chores had to do with sorting the potatoes by size. Trucks were loaded with bins marked small, medium, and large. The farmers charged a fee for the time it took to do all this painstaking work.

One day, Frank decided to throw all his potatoes on to the back of his truck without first sorting them by sizes. He just got on the road and headed for the market. The other farmers mocked him, judged him, and then later complained about him when they found out that he got paid the same amount as they did even though he hadn't sorted out his potatoes.

The owner of the market informed the others that Frank

did, indeed, show up with his potatoes sorted by size. When pressed for an explanation, Frank clarified the mystery. Instead of taking the smoothest and fastest road to the market, Frank took the bumpiest, most rocky road. In doing so, the potatoes got jostled around in the back of the truck. As they bounced and bumped, a natural course of action took place. The smallest potatoes fell to the bottom of the truck. The mediums sized potatoes landed in the middle. And, the largest potatoes rose to the top. By the time he got off the bumpy road, all of Frank's potatoes were where they needed to be.

In this book, I talk about the journey that comes before the results are achieved, about the bumpy road we travel while on the spiritual path. Power lies within our endurance, our persistence, our growing through the bumps and the bruises. In them, we find the seeds of our empowered spirits. Regardless of how shaky the ground might feel beneath our feet, at some point we stop resisting, we wake up, and we realize that all along, we were walking on sacred ground.

Tibetan Buddhist nun, teacher, author, Pema Chodron tells a story of five mountain climbers who set out on a long, high climb, together. Along the way, one stopped down at the bottom by a stream, and decided to stay there. Two made it mid way, and two made it to the top. Is there a winner here? Can't you learn just as much by the stream or mid way up a mountain as you can from the top? An empowered spirit knows that every step is in the right direction toward a divine destiny. An empowered spirit knows when to stop and rest, to sit by the stream, to be still. The journey is just as important and the final destination. If there is turbulence, so be it. Sometimes, you have to lose everything before you can take another step.

If you see this as a failure, as evidence that you cannot reach your goals, (or worse, that you're not worthy of them) then you will feel defeated. If you can see your losses as necessary, cleverly disguised blessings, then you will begin to feel/know the power of your journey.

Think of yourself as a Raven. This particular bird comes out to play in blizzards and hurricanes. It is the turbulence that gives it strength. No matter where you are, you are on sacred ground. Your path was designed in divine order. All you have to do is believe in yourself, believe in what you want to do, have an open heart to yourself and to the people you meet along the way. Be present to every moment, every step of the way.

I once thought I could avoid the aches of life by becoming a psychotherapist and later, a minister. I thought that if I could just help people to understand themselves while also being a kind, compassionate, spiritually-minded human being, I wouldn't having to suffer. I wanted my concept of altruistic goals to insulate me from all the unpleasant tasks of introspection and growing pains. No matter how hard I tried to hide, I couldn't run from the real work it takes to live a spiritually-centered life. More than just a knowing of theologies, scriptures, and words, the spirituals life is a daily dedication and an ongoing practice of spiritual principles. Regardless of the dogma we choose to follow, or the rituals we choose to perform, we cannot escape what is truly in our hearts. As our hearts purify and open, we focus on being centered in love and peace.

While on the road to finding this love and peace in my own heart, I made mistakes. I made so many mistakes, that it would be a sad turn of events to list them all here. Instead, I present a series of essays that flows with the stream of consciousness that tells the story of one person's journey. I stepped on to this road with my eyes half shut and resisted all that it took to see clearly, the light of a good and wonderful God. I wanted to turn back when the road got rough, but there was no where else to turn. As a result, I survived, and as the large potatoes in the truck, I would like to think that I've risen up a little bit closer to the top.

What follows are a series of stories and thoughts. Some are mine, some I borrowed and made mine, some have changed names and slightly changed circumstances. Most are mostly true. All were collected while on the spiritual path, the bumpy road to enlightenment.

You, too, rise to the top by not fearing the bumpy roads of your good and your not-so-good, by focusing on where you want to go and the type of person you want to be when you get there, by keeping your heart pure and your mind open. When the road finally smoothes, you'll be pleased and you'll be at peace. Let us pray that all people everywhere can live in peace. Let us pray to somehow, be instruments of that peace.

Chapter 1

The Journey Begins

My story

M y story begins with Catholicism. I attended Catholic school in Edison, New Jersey, for eight years, from first to eighth grade. It was there, in St. Matthews, that I built a foundation for an understanding of what it meant to have a God in one's life. Oddly enough, there was not a lot of talk about God, so much as there was a system of behavior control and management that was, supposedly, mandated by God and made known to us by way of the Sisters of Mercy.

I attended church regularly, received my first Holy Communion at about the age of nine, received the sacrament of Confirmation in sixth grade, and graduated in the eight grade. In between I was taught how to spell, how to speak with respect, and how to fear. On occasion, I considered being a nun, on other occasions, I considered being a priest, and on most occasions, I did as I was told. Since most of my neighbors and all of my cousins were also Catholic, I did not know of anything beyond the world of Catholicism. (also in my case, there was the integrated world of my Hispanic culture, so I had nothing to compare to and no reason to think that anything was different anywhere else.)

With graduation from St. Matthew's Catholic School, came the opportunity to make my first real choice about the direction of my life. I was given the choice between Catholic School and Public School. My brother, two years my senior, was already attending Public High School and seemed to be having a better time than some of the other kids I knew who were attending Catholic High School, so I went with the Public School option.

In public school, a whole new world presented itself. It was there I discovered the freedom to release pent-up feelings of oppression. I stopped going to church, I stopped behaving, I stopped being a good Catholic girl, and I grabbed at each and every chance to explore what it meant to be liberated. With adults assuming my continued "goodness", I was living a lot of "badness". By the time I graduated high school, I had gotten into enough trouble and enough dangerous situations to make up for all my years of restlessness. I found myself, eventually, feeling lost, scared, and unsure of what to do next. I decided to go on a search for a sense of belonging that had less to do with my wild side and more to do with where it all began. I went back to church.

It wasn't long before I realized that my search was going to have to take me somewhere beyond the Catholic school of my upbringing. I knew that there was something missing for me and that my experiences in the world, the experiences that were forming who I was becoming, let me in on a reality that was broader than the teachings of St. Matthew's. I didn't know what it was. I didn't know how to define it. But, I did know that there was something more I needed to learn.

I began what I called a search for truth beyond Catholicism. Staring with a new circle of friends, I began to explore churches that were in my town but that had been, previously, foreign to me. I perused, also, independent studies that took me into the sacred texts of various religions, to the great thinkers of philosophy, and to modern theorists of human behavior. I attended Gospel services, Baptist churches, Seventh Day Adventists, Jewish temples. In 1978, a large gathering of Pentecostal types met in the New Jersey Meadowlands and I came away from the event convinced that I had been "slain in the spirit" and took on the temporary role of born again Christian.

As a born-again Christian, I attended services that called for a lot of gospel singing and speaking in tongues. I had fun for a while and even considered becoming a Christian preacher. I took bible lessons and learned a lot more than I had in Catholic school about the actual teachings of the bible. I loved (and still love) prayer and I felt blessed by the Holy Spirit. But I didn't like being told who to vote for, what to think, or how to fulfill my role as a woman. I soon became disillusioned by the onslaught of judgment and hidden agendas that I noticed in the movement and I stepped away.

The next step on my spiritual journey had to do with the New Age and New Thought communities. It was there I discovered various meditation techniques and healing methods. I attended channelings, readings, and healing workshops. I was introduced to Tarot, I Ching, Yoga,

Paramahansa Yogananda, GuruMyi, Reikki, Unity Church, Science Of Mind, and The Course in Miracles.

In spite of all the learning that was of great interest and of great value, I continued to search for an answer to my questions of self. What is my purpose, who am I to be, what are the lessons of suffering, what is spiritual integrity, how do I live according to my own professed values, how do I find a god in my struggles? Hints presented themselves, but satisfactory eluded me.

In time and with consistent concentration on prayer and meditation, I found that the answer was within me, within my own access to higher consciousness and wisdom. I had been looking somewhere "out there" in the religions and philosophies of man-made dogma. I had been looking for someone or something to lead me, to answer me, to direct my path. With a sigh of relief and a new-found sense of responsibility for my own thoughts and behaviors, I came face to face with my own spirit. And in contacting this spirit, I dedicated myself to its growth.

There have been times when I've stepped outside of my deepest held beliefs, usually in the midst of some personal crisis, when I would look everywhere outside of myself for help and relief. It was during those times I suffered most. In one particular situation, I had failed at something important to me. Spirits were crushed and hearts were broken. With shame and guilt, I was forced into a period of extreme purging and catharsis. Suffering brought out the worst in me, before the best could be found. I left my life, as I had known it, kicking and screaming. I went into hiding. I fought against the changes that were shattering my world. The person I emerged as left behind a battered shell. I was tired and weary, but ready to resurrect.

I took my new steps tentatively. I made a commitment to

my physical, emotional, and spiritual healing. It was during this process that I discovered The New Seminary of Interfaith Ministers. Interfaith is a ministry of integration, of acceptance, and of inclusion. It is the path that makes sense to me because it looks for the similarities and the unifying principles of spirituality, as opposed to the discriminatory, ridged aspects of religious dogma.

In dedicating myself to a life of conscientious spiritual living, the challenge is for me to be in a constant state of heightened awareness of my own behavior, thoughts, and intentions. There are times when I think that it would be easier to regress to a time of reactionary life for the temporary satisfaction of relief from a moment of anger or angst. But then a prayer starts to ring in my head, as if a song from and angel, and I thank God for the patience it must take to complete me, to keep me on the path of completion, and to hold me dear, even in my moments of weakness.

I understand, now, that the direction of my spiritual journey is to serve as an Interfaith Minister, and I am thankful for the sacred blessing of this journey. As I read in a poem by the African poet Ntozake Shange: "I found God in myself and I loved her fiercely".

Ordination

Making the decision to become a minister came in the middle of a telephone call. I'd heard about people getting "the call" but I never imagined it could be so literal. But, there I was, having a phone conversation with a friend about the spiritual path, when I made the decision to attend seminary. It was a strange, yet exciting moment. A moment that would change my life. Previously, I'd never really given any serious consideration to seminary programs. I am a reformed academic snob. Having once believed that my next educational achievement would be a doctorate, I researched programs that would allow for movement back into the daily grind of work and school. What happened, instead, was a surprisingly comfortable decision to enter into a seminary program for Interfaith Ministries.

Tossing aside my reluctance to spend time and money on something that would not give me an academic degree, I made the decision based on a strong desire and commitment to make an overall improvement in my character. I had just begun the exiting of a particularly difficult time in my life, and wanted to know, deeply, that there was no turning back. In psychological terms, it might be said that I had experienced a breakdown of sorts. In metaphysical/archetypal terms, it might be said that I had been fighting my shadow side. In spiritual terms, it would have been referred to as a dark night of the soul. But, in my own terms, it was just plain old ugly, painful desperation.

Desperation has a way of making you feel as though you are a victim to an unfair, manipulative, devious, murderous plot to destroy your mental health. It is an extreme anxiety, a loss of hope, an angst-ridden, pitiful state of being. It would be truly tragic to survive such pathetic turmoil without having learned something big and important. For me, it was exactly what I needed in order to be shaken out of my self-centered sleep. I woke up and found the ministry.

I didn't know what I was going to do with a program of study that would have me make a commitment to a life based on spiritual principles, but I did know that I had long been searching for some sort of spiritual assurance, and I was ready to seek out the sacred.

I went into this knowing that I had many more questions than answers, especially when it came to the who, why, and what about the concept of a god. I compare what I want to believe now, as an adult on a spiritual path, to that of a scary, mean, father-god, the one I knew as a child in Catholic school. The messages we received as children, and I dare say especially as little girls, were so far beyond a child's ability to dispute.

There were a number of oppressive factors that were at work against our creating a sense of assertiveness, independence and autonomy. Social and cultural factors, as well as highly ridged religious dogma held us back from touching the center of our being. As an adult, I have had to struggle against that conditioning. I had to find a spiritual center that came from within, and that had little or nothing to do with the "out there" god of my childhood upbringing.

When I first contemplated the ministry, I was filled with a sense of unholy hypocrisy, like it was all just a little joke that I was playing on my psyche and that it was too unreal or too pompous to really allow myself full participation. But then, as the second year came to a close, and I was completing my required work, I began to find, within myself, a subtle switch to something I can only begin to explain as a feeling of humble gratitude. I began to feel honored, excited. I began to move away from the sudden urge to run away and say "oh no, I am an unworthy, bad person", to "I think I can love this." But mostly, I can testify that the worst of times always end, that blessings always lay shrouded behind painful transitions, and that prayers are always answered. Eventually. Somehow.

Chapter 2

Metanoia

M etanoia is word that has its origin in Greek, meaning "to change". There was a time in my life when I was literally dying for a change. I was in the process of suffering the consequences for having deeply hurt the person I loved most in life. Alone and feeling desperate, I wanted someone to rescue me, to relieve me of my terrorizing guilt and shame. I did not understand my own behavior nor did I understand the extent to which I was suffering. I felt as though I had been split in two, as if my insides were collapsing in on me. I was crashing, burning, falling apart, and headed at high speed towards self-destruction.

Passive suicide. When I heard the term, I knew it described my life. I was wasting away, having lost over 25 pounds from an already thin body. I hadn't eaten solid food in close to a month. Agoraphobia kept me from leaving the house for more than a few miles at a time. My depression was close to being debilitating, keeping me indoors and under covers for 3-4 days at a time.

The Bumpy Road To Enlightenment

One night, I got a 2:00 a.m. phone call from a stranger in Oregon. A friend of a friend. She'd heard the story I was so ashamed of and she decided to tell me that I was a worthless human being. When the phone rang, I was awake. At that time, I wasn't sleeping more than 45 minutes a night. Every night, throughout the night I would just lay in bed and devise suicide letters in my head, planning, planning. My best ideas were left lying beside me as scattered thoughts because I didn't have the strength to get up and write them down.

My plan was to call a friend who lived several miles from my home. I would call her and ask her to come by, when she had the time. By the time she got there, I would be dead. I would leave the front door open and a note on the dinning room table, advising her to call 911 and to not come in to the bedroom because my dead body would be there. On the note, I would have names of people for her to call, along with statements that would make it easier for them to handle the news. I would have her tell them that I had had a heart attack. I would ask her to call someone to take care of my bird and my cat. I had names and numbers listed in no particular order of priority.

It may have been delusional thinking, but in the night, it all made sense. My plan to escape the extensive emotional pain that was keeping me from food and work and friends and life. In the night, all I wanted was the strength to carry out my plan. In the day, I would walk through a cloud of depression and confusion, barely capable of conversation.

At work, I closed the door to my office and searched my mind for yet another excuse to leave. One day, while sitting at my desk, I passed out from not having eaten in several days. An employee found me and took me taken to the hospital where they diagnosed me as being malnourished and suggested I consider seeing a therapist for depression.

On another day at work, where I served as the administrator of a mental health clinic, I heard screaming out in the hallway. A man had come in to our building who was clearly psychotic and potentially dangerous. Someone called the police and everyone cleared the lobby. I got up from my desk and slowly walked down the hall to see him. He turned his head and watched me approach while continuing his stream of profanities and frantic, desperate, almost primal screams. My staff tried to stop me, implored me to stay away from him. But there was something in his eyes, something I understood. As we stood face to face, he said "do you know who I am?" I shook my head no and he went on to tell me things I knew weren't true, but that he in his madness, believed. In my mind I was thinking: "Something I do know to be true is the fact that the only difference between you and me, is that I'm not screaming out loud."

Then came that 2:00 a.m. Oregon caller who started her tirade by telling me that I was a worthless human being. Her voice increased in volume every time I tried to interrupt her barrage of insults. She cursed at me, called me ugly names, told me that I was no good, wondered why I was still alive. I listened to her.

I was filled with self-loathing and I wanted to hear all that she had to say, all the unkindness, all the damnation of my soul. In my heart, I agreed with her. She gave me the strength I needed to carry out my comforting, late-night plans.

It takes only a moment to lose the natural instinct for survival, and in that moment, a person can decide to die. In that moment, the best laid plans for the future are set aside. Suddenly, life-long dreams have no life and there is no hope to hold on to. In living that kind of moment, I hung up the phone, got up from my bed, and shook off the dreaded drain of depression's restraint. I got up in spite of the heaviness in my head and in my limbs. I walked to the kitchen and I pulled out the blender. In the blender, I poured two cans of a vitamin-rich chocolate drink, the only link I'd had to nutrition in several days. I then added the contents of four different prescription medications, a variety of anti-depressants and anti-anxiety trials that had, on occasion, provided temporary relief from my suffering. For good measure, I added two bottles of over the counter sleeping pills, and Hershey's syrup for taste. The sound of the blender's swirl was eerily comforting. I remember resting my head against the cold glass when I turned off the motor.

I decided to prepare my body for its death by lighting an Indian ceremonial smudge stick. I wasn't sure what to do with it, so I just stood there holding it, in a daze. I found it hard to breathe, to think, to move. I stood there, paralyzed by grief. I decided not to write a letter. It seemed too difficult, too tiring. I was ready. I poured the concoction into a glass and took a sip. A tiny sip. The phone rang. I ignored it. It rang again. I ignored it. It rang and it rang and it rang until it was as if it were getting louder and screaming out my name. Finally, I put down the glass, ran across the room, and cried out in to the phone.

What followed were a series of divine interventions. God sent friends, teachers, preachers, books, ways and means for me to deeply change from the inside out, to shift my soul from an ego-centered focus to an intense, internal, spiritual focus. The death I experienced was of an old self, an old way of being. I found direction, learned ways to address and correct my areas of weakness, looked with rigorous honesty at my life and how I had been living it. I humbly submitted to the comprehensive introspection I needed to do in order to make a commitment, to take a vow, and to live in a new way. What I lost I could not get back. But what I've found I can never replace.

The Phoenix Rises

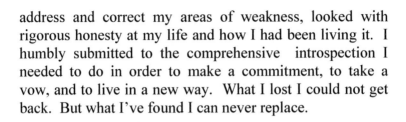

If only it all could have changed at the snap of a finger. But the road is bumpy because the bumps serve a purpose in challenging us, grooming us, creating strength and endurance and conviction within us. Crawling out from under the depression I had suffered took time. I was ending my first year of seminary, and I could finally see clearly, the light of my spirit, the promise of a path that could only lead to goodness. I was hopeful, excited. And yet, there were times when I doubted. I began to look for consistent reassurances. And assuredly, the universe provided.

All major religions and philosophies tell us that the human plight is made of dichotomies, and paradoxes, ying and yang, up and down, dark and light. It's not that we can escape our suffering, but that our approach to suffering, our attitudes, our behaviors, our thoughts are all factors that create the final outcome of each and every circumstance of our lives. With this in mind, I acknowledged my need for an adjusted perspective and I began to pray for a shift in my thinking.

In psychology, we approach depression by looking at organic and/or situational factors. From a spiritual perspective, we approach depression by looking at areas in need of correction. In my case, what was in need of correction was my own negative self-image. The prayer I used to start my process of correction was an Islamic chant I had learned in seminary. The words of the chant say: "There is no God but God". I asked myself, what was I making more important than my spiritual path? What was I making into a god? Who was I making more important than God? With each question, I looked at the extent to which faulty thinking had contributed to my problematic sense of worth. I was feeling reluctant to call myself a minister, afraid to fill the robes and the role, feeling unworthy, feeling like an imposter. I wanted to know that I was on the right path and that I was the right person to have answered that call to spiritual service. I changed my prayer to a request for direction, support, and clarity.

Within a few days, I received a call from a guy I know who occasionally joined in at a clergy discussion group that I belong to. He asked if I would be intersected in attending a clergy leadership conference that he was coordinating. I said yes and looked forward to an interfaith networking opportunity. I went to the conference, but I got bored about half way through and considered making up an excuse to leave early. It was a beautiful Saturday afternoon, and my attention span has never been known to behave all that well when I have to sit still for long periods of time. Luckily, I met an interesting conversationalist who held my attention throughout lunch and up to when they announced the keynote speaker.

I knew I couldn't get up and leave while the keynote speaker was addressing the crowd, so I resigned myself to staying for another hour. As it turned out, the speaker had a lot more to say that an hour's worth of notes. He spoke well in to the afternoon and in spite of myself, I was captivated. He was intense and passionate in his message. He inspired me, humbled me, lifted my spirits. I even stopped looking out the window and paid close attention. I was glued to his every word, grateful to have stayed put.

At some point in his presentation, he asked us all to stand. With conviction and passion, he told us that we were chosen, beloved children of God and that we had a mission, that we were there on that day to know, to deeply know, that we were, indeed, chosen. He kept saying it and saying it and I wanted so much to believe him. Having served as a chaplain at Ground Zero for a few days after the terrorist attack on the World Trade Center, he drew an analogy and told us that we too had been broken and shattered, but that now it was time for us to be re-built so that we could be stronger than ever, so that we could now accomplish what we had been chosen to do. He said that we were to rise up, like the phoenix from its ashes, so that we could do great things. He just kept repeating himself and my heart longed to belief that he was talking to me and to know, in my heart, that everything he was saying was true.

I wanted, so badly, to believe and so I started praying to hear it, to really hear God calling my name through the speaker. I wanted to really, really, really know that I had been chosen. I wanted to know that what he was saying was true and that it was meant for me. So then he said "I know you want God to call out your name, and so I'm telling you that God is calling out your name!" And I thought : "Wow, that's amazing. That's what I wanted to hear. Sort of. But, what if he's talking about all these other people and not to me, specifically?" It seemed as though I just could not be satisfied, even though I wanted to be. I just had to know, deeply.

What happened next is the kind of thing that turns an ordinary day into to a miracle. There were about 125 clergy people in attendance at this conference, many of whom are big names in their communities. The keynote speaker knew many of them, personally and most of them by reputation. He called out some of those big names and asked them to come up on stage with him. He said he wanted about 5 or 6 other ministers to join him in leading the larger group in prayer. What happened next, amazes me to this day. To my great delirious joy, as I stood there praying for a sign, he called out my name.

I'd never met this man before. I'd never seen him or heard of him, But for some reason, he stood there and called out: "Reverend Lori Cardona." I didn't hesitate. I moved, quickly and directly, up on to the stage to a space next to him, as if it had been planned. Out of all those ministers in the room, only 6 of us were called up and I was one of them. Called by my name. He asked each of us to take a turn at the microphone, to say a prayer. In a state of amazement, I did as he asked and prayed over the crowd while all the other ministers bowed their heads, held hands, and swayed to the soft , instrumental version of a peace song. And then, I knew.

Embracing change

There are times when we initiate a change in our lives that fills us with excitement and anticipation. We look forward to a new job, a new place to live, a new relationship. Although there may be some nervousness or hesitation, the overall feeling is one of confidence and renewal. Then, there are those changes that are thrust upon us and which throw us into panic, fear, a sense of loss, of losing control, losing a dream. We lose a job that gave us a sense of purpose and identity, as well as financial security. A lover who we once believed would join us into old age leaves us. We are devastated, we suffer unwelcome and unbearable angst. We change, in our pain, we don't recognize ourselves, we don't even recognize the new way in which we are forced to live. We question our ability to adjust.

A quote attributed to Neitzche, states: "You must be ready to burn yourself in your own flame. How could you become new if you had not first become ashes?" Is it possible to believe in the phoenix we will rise to become when we are in the ashes? We look for our former avenues of comfort, but where are the friends who fell out during the fallout? Bonds you once thought you could depend on are broken. This is especially true and especially painful during a relationship's break up, when friendships once thought solid shift with the tides and decide that they cannot be neutral. How do you cope? How do you rise from the ashes? How do you embrace the change?

During times of difficult transition, embracing change sounds like an oxymoron. In exploring our transitions, we stand in front of what might be, initially, an unpleasant mirror in which to look. We see, possibly for the first time, our fears, our areas of resistance, our dysfunctional behaviors, and maybe even our addictive tendencies. We sit in a fog and try to see clearly. What is there to embrace?

I recently co-facilitated a workshop on this topic of adjusting to, and embracing frightening change. We asked our participants to identity the opportunities found during times of painful change. We all agreed that, even in the midst of our trials, there was a flicker of hope, an inner knowing of sorts that peeked into our troubled time. We discussed the fact that, because of our pain, we began a journey to an enlightenment of self, of heightened awareness, of movement toward positive changes. Books appeared that spoke to us as unseen guides, new friends presented themselves as gifts, spiritual comforts began to emerge and settle in as permanent guests. We began to grow toward a way of being that seemed strangely suitable to an emerging stronger self.

As suffering begins to diminish in its scope, we rejoice in our survival. We become wiser, more empathic. We begin to laugh and to dance again. We develop improved images of ourselves, and we like what we see. We've asked ourselves the hard questions of our lives. What do I truly believe in, about myself, about the ways in which I cope, about what I want, about what I don't want, about what I am willing to change? We ask ourselves if we are willing, and ready, to do all that is necessary to take ourselves from the depth of despair to the zenith of a blessing once disguised.

Detachment

In her novel, *By The Light Of My Father's Smile*, Alice Walker shares her wisdom in telling us: "When life descends into the pit, I must become my own candle, willingly burning myself to light up the darkness around me." I want to be my own candle. I got to thinking that what I really needed to do was to work harder at detaching from my ego. I figured that, as a detached, compassionate witness to my life, changes and bumps along the road wouldn't end up feeling like devastations or failures. They'd be lessons learned and grist for the mill of spiritual growth. I wanted to light up the darkness around me, but I needed help. I searched out and found a retreat center, not far from my home that just so happened to be conducting a four-day intensive on the concept of detachment.

So, I showed up at the retreat center and there were all these people with serene expressions of contentment on their faces. I was a little intimidated, but I was on a quest to share in their serenity. I listened to them, closely. I compared their stories to mine. I learned to differentiate between detachment as an act of escape and detachment as an act of loving-kindness. We were told that, according to many eastern philosophies and precepts, detachment is an accomplishment that allows for relief from suffering.

We are to cultivate a witness of sorts, an aspect of ourselves that watches our dramas unfold without feeding the ego's need to control. I had to wonder if it was possible to do so without packing in the real world and moving to an ashram. I also wondered if anyone would notice my apprehension when it came time to share a bit of my reason for being there. I took the microphone and spoke of a desire to detach from certain unpleasant ego aspects that had managed to creep in and become a part of me. At best, I said, I would like to detach from some aspects of my history. I looked down to see if my umbilical cord was hanging out, exposed, as I spoke of a hunger that seemed, temporarily, nameless. Others acknowledged that there was indeed, a mysterious craving for a place to attach, to plug in the cord, to feel complete. And yet, we were there to learn the art of detachment.

As the weekend went on, I was able to identify the mysterious craving. What I was beginning to see more clearly, was a dichotomy that called for an integration of a splintered self. I had become attached to a list of "shoulds" that were creating obstacles to my own progress and growth. I was stuck in a story of how it should be.

To detach from our "shoulds" is one step toward moving through the obstacles that were created by them. In an attempt to apply this concept, I began to pay less attention to the drama of a particular moment, and more attention to my own thinking, the beliefs I had become attached to, the value I had placed on the not-always-kind opinion of others, the words I used, in my head and aloud. I began to witness the ego attachments, the areas of pride that had hardened my heart to others, and the areas of shame, that had hardened my heart to myself. I began to work on the integration of a new belief system, one that contradicted the old ego-laden tapes. I began to feel a gentle releasing of old, negative influences, ways of living and thinking once thought to be essential to my survival. It began to make sense. A lesson from The Course In Miracles tells us: "Every thought you have makes up some segment of the world you see. It is with your thoughts, then, that we must work, if your perception of the world is to be changed."

So often we see our obstacles as those things that are out there, those people, those circumstances. We often forget that, even in the worst of circumstances, we are, at the very least, in control of the way in which we move through them. . As we learn to detach from our demand that our story unfold as we once thought it should, we make allowances for gentle acceptance, and we take responsibility for our part in the creation of what has become our reality. In his book, *Deep Is The Hunger*, Howard Thurman shares these provocative thoughts: "My ego is like a fortress. I have built its walls stone by stone. But I have stayed here long enough. I relax the barriers. I abandon all that I think I am. I let go of the past. I withdraw my grasping hand from the future. And, in the great silence of this moment, I rest my soul".

Identity

On a recent vacation from Miami to New York, I sat on a local transit train en route to Penn Station and wondered what it would be like to be the train conductor. I watched him as he watched us, his passengers, as he called out our destinations, came by to take our tickets, as he swept his eyes over book covers and newspaper headlines. I wondered if he was doing what he wanted to do. I wondered if his highly polished uniform buttons were a source of pride. I wondered what he dreamed of when he was a little boy.

Later in the day, while walking along on the streets of Manhattan, I found myself questioning the dreams of the people who caught my eye. The woman in front of me at "Grays Papaya" reminded me of someone I once knew, which had me making assumption about her role in life. The well-perfumed, well-dressed young women were, in my mind, perusing an identity through newly acquired career positions. The even better dressed were perusing identities in other ways, each of which I made up, depending on their walk, their eyes, their mannerisms. All assumptions, on my part, all questions of identity. Who are they? Who am I?

Violin players with donation cups were performing on New York subway station corridors, looking contented and engrossed in their music. As I stood and watched them, I became aware that I was holding my breath, floating with their soothing sound, dreaming of sitting with them, of re-creating myself, for myself. I searched my pocket for a dollar, and as I straightened up from the donation cup, my eyes were held by one of the musicians. I felt so grateful for the subtle smile, the tilt of his head in recognition. As we saw each other, in that moment, I had a glimpse of my own self.

As I continued on my way, I noticed that winter coats in New York have changed from my younger days. Everyone seems to be so fashionably bundled. I began to think of their coats as uniforms, identifiers of social class, economic status, statements of youth or culture, statements of desire for recognition of achievement or direction. I began to think of the layers needed for warmth in winter clothing as analogous to the layers of resistance and fear we accumulate over the years, the layers of distraction away from our original self.

The original self is the one who first allowed for the most extravagant of dreams and imaginings. A child is filled with questions and wonder. She has creative thoughts and moments of inspiration that allow her to express herself as anyone and anything she imagines herself to be. But then a message is given, a message of "you can't do that, you shouldn't". And the first layer is put in place, the layer of suppression. She begins to ignore, block, deny her dreams. Layers accumulate. She puts on a lack of belief in herself, she begins to harden around the sweet excitement of her imaginings. Maybe the final layer is a complacency that allows for forgetting, for the total loss of her original dream.

The bumpy road to enlightenment serves as a way for us to break away from the self-imposed restrictions of our past. We grow up, take responsibility for our own lives and stop using the old, negative messages as magnets to attract others who continue to perpetuate our vulnerable, victim stance. Being forced into change and stripped of everything we know allows for the re-birth of our original self, our true identity, and as an added blessing, the opportunity to pursue our most deeply imagined dreams.

I think back to a time when I had been stripped of the identity I once thought defined me. I'd lost my job and my long-term relationship within a 6 month period. I had to look at myself as a separate entity, separate from a role in an agency, separate from a role in a relationship. I had to come face to face with the rawness of my being, a person without a label to lean on. My changing life was changing the direction of my dreams and I was left with nothing more than my own resources, and the entire universe. I took one step. The universe did the rest. I look back in awe and in wonder. I give thanks.

Chapter 3

Trust and Faith

The Blessing Of Renewal

I n taking the step toward beginning a new life, I had to step out in faith. I had to trust the process of renewal. I had to let go of the past by believing in my own ability to create a spiritually focused future. I wrote: "I Trust In God" on the scrolling marquee of my computer screen, and I called a Realtor. I'd decided that for me, letting go had to be literal, thorough, and complete. I was going to sell my house.

In preparing to leave my home, I did what so many movers do. I had a yard sale. As I watched my memories get sold and sent away for just a few dollars each, a strange twist in my sentiments began. I found that the more I got rid of, the less I wanted. Little by little, I added more and more of my past life to the present life of strangers. I realized, as the sale went on into the late afternoon, that the decision to let go of the house was actually a decision to let go of the attachment I had to the life I had once lived there. I began to imagine that I could leave, unscathed, with no more than a backpack and a toothbrush.

As it turned out, I needed to fill a storage room with boxes of treasured books and a few miscellaneous items, but essentially gave away, sold, or just threw away a household full of "stuff". As I looked over the things that once described who I was, I gave myself to the memories and feelings. I looked back, sat with yesterday, and struggled to let it all go. I couldn't leave unscathed, as I had hoped. I needed to feel the pain of this transition in order to truly heal from any perceived losses. So much of who I used to be lived in the walls and in the "things" that lived with me there.

One of the things I sold at the yard sale was a special ring. That ring, at one time represented a relationship that was supposed to last forever. On the day of my yard sale, an elderly man stopped by and looked around for something to take home to his wife. As we spoke, he told me the story of a marriage that was in its 35th year, one that had seen sacrifice, poverty, and hardship in exchange for the college education of their two sons. The youngest son had just recently moved out and off to school, leaving the couple with an opportunity to spend time alone and to spend some of their savings on themselves. He told me of a vacation that they had been planning on but wouldn't take. His wife, it turned out, was now very ill and would soon die of emphysema. He told me that, instead of waking up and thinking about a future with her, he woke up and leaned over to see if she was still alive.

I looked around the yard to see if there was something I could give him, to take to her. In an impulsive act of purging, I gave him the ring. The ring no longer held its promise to me. But maybe it could continue to live out its original purpose by keeping that man's promise to love his wife until the day she died. He told me that he was going to go home and put the ring on his wife's finger. Our eyes met in a moment of knowing that she would die with the ring on her finger, and that its intended, original purpose, would indeed, be held as a sacred covenant.

The reason why I needed to go to such a great length to de-materialize, was because the process, to me, symbolized the internal, emotional, and spiritual cleansing that I was doing in conjunction with the move. As I inventoried the contents of my home, so did I do an inventory of myself, of my character, my way of being. Some things just needed to go. So as odds and ends were taken and faded from my sight, I imagined the packing of my pride and my ego, boxed and carried away. I sat on the stoop and said goodbye.

And so it was that the move out of a house became an opportunity to move into a willingness of renewal. We don't have to wait for life-changing events to motivate us into introspection and renewal. Just as we don't have to wait until Spring to do our spring-cleaning. People who abide by the precepts of the 12-step recovery program understand this by way of a grueling but necessary fourth step. The fourth step states that "we made a searching and fearless moral inventory of ourselves." What a difficult, courageous thing to do, to look inside and to be rigorously honest with yourself as to what you find in the dark corners of your own psyche. And then, to work towards changing/transforming those things that we see and understand to be obstacles to our spiritual growth.

Its so easy to not look, to be distracted away from the responsibility we have to our own spiritual growth. How

much easier it is took outside of ourselves, to pad our egos
with people, substances, and activities that allow us the
quick fixes of distraction away from any unpleasant
characteristics that we'd rather not own. We are afraid to
be in the silence of our inner worlds. And yet, the silence
screams out loud when the fixes fall away and we are
forced to face our own selves, raw and exposed. If we are
going to attain our highest good, if we are going to become
the spiritual beings we were born to be, then we need to
break free of un- fulfilling ways of being, destructive habits
or addictions, grudges that imprison us in the past, acts of
unkindness (towards others as well as towards ourselves).
This process of transformation, from an ego-centered to a
spirit-centered way of being, begins with no more than the
willingness to do so.

Like the butterfly that cannot fly in its full form of
beauty without the struggle of metamorphosis, so too do we
have to challenge ourselves. The step we take into the
unknown abyss of change requires that we trust a process
that promises a new place to live once we leave the comfortable home we once knew. The home of ego-laden
living has its comforts, yes, just as the cocoon is
comfortable for the caterpillar. But to fly like a butterfly, is
to be free to explore the heights and the depth of our
potential. In her book, *Woman Awake*, Christina Fledman
states "To move from darkness into light, we need to be
willing to embrace the twilight, the time of disillusionment
with ourselves, the chaos and the disorder"

We become enriched with spiritual enthusiasm when we
allow ourselves a time of transformation and renewal, a
time of spring cleaning for our souls. We do this by
maintaining an awareness of our own selves, our intentions,
our willingness to be improved, by forgiving ourselves for

our imperfections and by forgiving others for theirs. We do
this by understanding that we can only grow spiritually
when we let go of the distractions that inhibit our spiritual
growth. When we do this, we arrive at a place of peace, a
home of comfort, trust, and faith. It is as we read in (a very
amended version) a poem by C. Tillery Banks:
"No more ugly days for me, the sun always shines, and the
rain is washing my gutters clean. Problems will only be
challenges. Disappoint will be growth because it will
teach me to choose more carefully. Delays will be lessons
in patience because I know that everything comes in time,
on time. If anything goes, I give it away and bless whoever
got it. Glory, Glory, Glory, Even my pain's gonna be
pretty."

Trust

At a church service I attended recently in Charlotte, NC
the preacher suddenly interrupted his own message to start
singing "We shall overcome." Within seconds, everyone
was on their feet and signing along. Voices were loud and
filled with conviction. We shall overcome. I thought about
how so many individual stories were attached to the people
around me as they sang with tears in their eyes. Each and
every story had painful aspects that needed to be solved,
healed, overcome. Singing with conviction is a prayer
called out for what we know to be true; that there is an end
to our suffering, there is an answer to our questions, there is
a light that shines through the darkness.

Many years ago, long before the invention of Prozac,
my friend Lou suffered a great deal with an obsessive-

compulsive disorder. At the time, there wasn't a commonly known name for it, so people just thought he was crazy. He couldn't understand what was happening to him, he just knew that there were certain things that he couldn't stop thinking about, worrying about, checking on. He eventually began to feel as though he were no longer capable of managing his own life. As he struggled daily, he was often told by others to just stop his irrational thinking and behavior, to snap out of it.

One day, a friend of his was watching a segment on a talk show that focused on anxiety disorders. A specialist from the National Institute of Mental Health was talking about an extreme form of anxiety know as Obsessive Compulsive Disorder. The friend called Lou and told him to call the show, which he did. He was directed to a specialist right there in his own hometown. Scared as he was, he made an appointment and went in for treatment.

What allowed Lou to survive between the suffering and the relief was an inner sense of trust in a process of overcoming. From a book called "Navigating The Future", by Mikela and Philip Tarlow, we are told of the Tibetan concept of Bardo, the place of in-between, of waiting. It is similar to the "In The Meantime" place that Iyanla Vanzant speaks of in her proposal that we maintain a certain introspective, heart-felt quality existence during times of seeming lack. The idea is to trust that this time in between goals, relationships, jobs, or whatever you're waiting for, is a time of necessary gestation for your soul's growth. The discomfort we feel when we don't know what's next is like the discomfort a pregnant woman feels when going through physical and hormonal changes. The life that grows inside her is like the new life that we are giving birth to within ourselves. We trust that, like the pregnant woman,

46

our discomfort is time-limited and that the end result will be worth the wait.

In a situation that has no end in sight, we can trust that there is a power greater than anything we can imagine which steps in by way of messages through friends, music, books, or ideas that seem to spring forward from nowhere. My friend Lou is a perfect example. While tortured by his own relentless obsessions, someone was watching a television show that had an answer. Coincidence? I don't think so. Just as I don't know how to explain the biological enzyme changes that occur when I am in the process of digesting foods, I cannot explain what metaphysical changes occur while I am waiting, in trust, for the answers during life-altering times. But just as surely as I trust that my food will be digested, I trust that my answers will come.

The answer will come by way of a mystical occurrence or by way of a mundane messenger. All we have to do is wait, and trust. If we are anxiously trying to control the outcome, we are like the man in his garden who finds a cocoon and tries to force the caterpillar in to a butterfly. The butterfly cannot overcome its discomfort in the cocoon by being forced out of its caterpillar stage. It overcomes by surrendering to the process and by trusting the natural order of its metamorphosis. And so it is with us. We trust. We overcome. We grow. We are blessed.

Faith

I used to suffer from panic attacks and generalized anxiety. I spent a lot of my anxiety-free time in fear of my

47

next panic attack. It occurred to me, somewhere around the middle of my second year of seminary, that it would be just too awful to live out my calling as an anxiety-ridden minister. I feared that my congregation would be made up of a group of codependent caregivers who would pacify my self-absorption by constantly reminding me that some of the greatest minds in history were tortured. They would protect me from strangers, make up excuses for my tardiness or absent-mindedness, and they'd learn to carefully indulged my every neurosis while whispering in to the telephone: "Oh, I'm so sorry, but Reverend Cardona won't be in today, she's home nurturing her agoraphobia" .

No, I didn't want to live that way. I began to pay close attention to how I was praying, what I was concentrating on, what I was thinking about myself, what I truly believed in. I came to understand what I was told by a minister some time ago, that we don't get what we pray for, we get where we pray from. If we think and pray from a mindset of fear, then we will be fearful. We cannot just pray for the fear to go away. We have to approach challenges that put us in fear's face by looking and leaping, moving into and past the discomfort, the urge to run away, the inner pull that tells us to do the same thing we've done before, the very same thing that didn't work but felt familiar. One very good place to start is in our most intimate relationships. It is here where we are most challenged. People come into our lives to be our teachers, our gurus, our opportunities to transform our character defects, our dysfunctional patterns, and ultimately, our souls.

Joe and Rita were a couple who came in to see me for counseling. They had entered into their relationship with an agreement to do things differently than each had done in the past, in previous relationships. Their past relationships were casebook studies in what not to do. They looked back, objectively, as if graduate students reviewing their completed curriculum. Armed with good intentions they set out to define and live out a "healthy relationship". What happened is what often happens with good intentions. You may have heard that the road to hell is paved with these meaningful plans. That's because they are not enough. The action that follows the plan is what tells you the truth.

So when Joe and Rita were faced with their discomforts, they laid down their very best of intentions and picked up the weapons of war. Fighting is a couple's way of not changing, of keeping a tight hold onto the need to be right, the need to blame, the need to mistrust, the need to judge. In her book *Awakening In Time*, Jacquelyn Small tells us that, for transformation to take place, for a person to become enlightened, her mind "must die to its old and outworn ways." In Buddhism, there is the idea that we have been hypnotized to believe in a certain way and that at some point we must be de-hypnotized in order for the mind to abandon its negative, defensive assumptions. A Christian scripture (Romans 12:2), tells us that we can be "transformed by the renewing of our mind".

This means resisting the urge to point the finger at others, the urge to be judgmental, to be unkind. It means having faith that, once you do it differently, you will indeed be different. Buddhist Monk Thich Nhat Hanh says that lashing out in anger, for example, is like seeing that your house is on fire and leaving it to burn while you run around looking for the person who lit the match. His advice for anger is that you take time to be mindful, to breathe through your discomfort, to have faith in your ability to do so. Your reward will be the realization that your discomfort has been transformed. The fire has been extinguished.

During a heated argument in their apartment, Joe walked out the door and headed towards the elevator. He had things to do, and places to go. But he was angry and had a compelling need to be vindicated. Inside the apartment, Rita was relieved and impressed. She was glad to see that Joe could walk away, perhaps to go calm down so that they could be ok later on in the day. But then, she heard footsteps returning. Instead of making it to the elevator, Joe was coming back in for an extended fight. Rita found herself praying "Go to the elevator, Joe, go to the elevator. Tell him, God, to go to the elevator. If he walks away, goes away for a while, then maybe things will change and we will be ok. But if he comes back in and yells at me, then………." . And then the key in the door. Joe says he couldn't stop himself. His good intentions had not been set to a discipline of mindfulness and faith. Without the transforming of his mind, there was no expansion of his heart.

I thought about this story as I set out to transform my anxiety to faith. Anxiety, anger, doubt, fear, and other painfully uncomfortable emotions are indicators of an absence of faith in the ultimate successes that we are entitled to. And so, I began to pray differently. Instead of praying for relief from my anxiety, I prayed to be more loving. As I began to feel the shift that comes with answered prayer, time passed , anxiety dissolved, and my heart began to opened more. My prayers have changed once again. I've begun to just say thank you. Thank you for this path, thank your for the many blessings. As I replace fear with faith, I am given more reasons to be thankful.

Fun

The other night I had a dream about the Dalai Lama. He was sitting in a room surrounded by a crowd of miniature versions of himself. He was smiling, like he does in all the photos we see of him, and all the little, miniature Dalai Lamas were smiling, too. Everyone looked exactly alike, and they all went from smiling to laughing and then back to smiling. Their laughter was full and hearty, the kind that makes your head fall back while you hold your stomach and burst out with a big and noisy "ha, ha, ha".

When I woke up I tried to figure out what I had missed, like what was making them laugh so much, and why did they do everything in perfect unison. Later that day, I came across a line from a daily meditation book called "A Woman's Spirit".   It caught my attention in light of the dream I had just had because it said: "I must be willing to chuckle many times today."   I began to think about laughter, giggles, chuckles, and humor, about people I know who love to laugh, and about people I know who generally seem to withhold laugher. I think I like the laughers best.   Laughers seem to see humor in situations that the more serious and morbid-minded among us don't see.   I think I'd like to be more of a laugher.

We often take ourselves too seriously. Way too seriously, we look at our lives, our relationships, our dramas.

We sigh in self-pity when troubled times tamper with our sense of safety and security. If someone dares to remind us that "someday you'll look back on this and laugh", we believe we've just been given license to threaten bodily harm. We get so self-absorbed, so concentrated on the hard times. We find it too difficult to take a step away, to take a moment of retreat and distance, in order to see the opportunity, the potential for spiritual grow, the learning. And perhaps, even, the humor.

Many years ago, when I was living in Greenville, SC, I started getting up a 6am to watch a yoga class on TV. Yoga had not reached the level of American popularity that it enjoys today, so I was having a hard time finding a local yoga class. One evening, while in a local neighborhood video store, I found a yoga instruction video in the sale's bin. To this day, and after many years of yoga instruction and instructors, it is still my favorite yoga class. Alan Finger, the instructor, presents an approach to yoga and spiritual enlightenment that I rarely see. The video is very well done, with great scenery both indoors and out, beautiful participants, and even a hint of eroticism. Throughout the class, Finger reminds us to enjoy ourselves and to remember that "Enlightenment isn't serious".

This is not to say that times don't get tough and that people don't suffer, or that we can easily detach from the waves we're forced to ride. But it is to say that the road to enlightenment can be taken with lighter steps. We can, indeed, learn to be less focused on our suffering, to stop romanticizing our suffering selves. It has been said that Buddha, while teaching the Four Noble Truths, taught that pain is inevitable but that suffering is optional. We decide how much of our precious life-energy will be spent in the suffering over a person or a situation. We decide how much we want to identify with our pain.

But, how do we see humor in suffering or laugh along with a Universe that giggles in cosmic delight at the child-like innocence of its inhabitants? Don't we do the same thing when we watch children angst at something that we know is trivial and benign? Perhaps all in life is no more than the change in perceptions we acquire as we moved from childhood concerns to adult concerns, and then on to concerns of the soul, concerns so much more rich and nourishing than those of the destitute ego. So, what do we do? In the same mediation book mentioned earlier, another passage leads us towards an answer. It says: "When we loosen our grasp on our concerns, there is room for the spiritual essence of all life to move through us in such a way that healing occurs." This brings us, again, to a question of trust. Are we willing to trust this statement? Are we willing to recognize and acknowledge what experience has already taught us?

What we create or exaggerate in our lives is whatever we keep our focus on. If the focus is on our troubles, then our hearts become filled with the sorrows associated with those troubles. When we change our focus, we open ourselves up to a change in our thinking. When we change our thinking, we change our feelings. As our feeling change, so do our behaviors and ultimately, our experiences. It is a law of the universe that is undisputed.

Perhaps the laughing Dalai's in my dream were trying to remind me of this, of the importance of maintaining a lightens of being, of not taking anything too seriously, lest we forget that we are not here to be so concerned with our ego selves. Perhaps all those multiple, identical Dalai Lama's in miniature were reminders of our unity. We are all the same, all one, all united on the journey of the same path, no one bigger or more important than the other. We are sisters, and Dalai Lama's and friends. We are here to laugh at life, rise to greatness of spirit, to smile a lot, and to enjoy.

Chapter 4

Love

Love Conquers Fear

I n the early fall of 1963, I was seven years old and very little for my age. I wore a very little, green plaid uniform, a very little forest green knee socks, a little white blouse, and a very big expression of terror on my face. It was my first day of Catholic school. I don't know how I got there or how I survived the day. There are only two thing I remember clearly. The first is that I was preoccupied with not having a peeing accident. As a first grader in a new school, I wanted very much to make a good first impression. This was, after all, the school my big brother went to, the one to which I had to ride a bus with the big kids, and where I would prove myself to be a worthy soldier in God's Roman Catholic Army of children. The year before, in kindergarten, the pressure wasn't so great. I was just a kid, then. However, on my first day there, I peed in my seat. So, on this first day, this first day of the rest of my catholic school days, (which at the time seemed like the rest of my life), I was very scared.

The second thing I remember is sitting in the cafeteria waiting for someone to call my name. We were told to sit quietly until our names were called. When you heard your name, you were to go to the front of the room and stand directly behind the person whose name was called before you. After all the names were called, we were told, a Sister Of Mercy would take us to our classroom. When my name was called, my full bladder and I walked slowly and carefully to the front of the room. I looked to the nun who had called my name and tried to plead with her, with silent desperate eyes, so that she would know that I was, indeed, a good girl who just had to go pee or else I would absolutely be walking faster, as per her request.

I walked, in my new starched green plaid uniform, to where she was standing in her new starched   black and white habit. We both looked very new and fresh, I thought. I smiled at her, in solidarity, and turned to stand behind the person in front of me, as instructed. Sister reached over, grabbed the sleeve of my little blouse and gave it a hard, sharp jerk, which yanked me out of my space and moved me over by about 8 inches. She then reminded me, via a microphone that transmitted her voice and my humiliation throughout the world, that her instructions were for me to stand directly behind the person in front of me. All the other children would have to wait until I stood correctly.

For the next eight years, I kept a wary eye out for the ever-present possibility of punishment while learning how to read, spell, and diagram sentences. Not much changed from year to year other than the size of my green plaid uniform and the extent to which I would, on occasion, challenge parochial scare tactics. By the time I returned to public school, in ninth grade, I was ready to break every rule and to rebel against my fear's restraints. I was running wild, and yet, running scared. I had been taught how to fear.

Teaching, parenting, governing, and controlling by way of fear is not specific to any one group. This mistaken and unkind approach has been used for centuries, as a world-wide phenomenon. In her book, *Return To Love*, Marianne Williamson refers to it as "Our individual and collective hells, a world that seems to press on us from within and without, giving false testimony to anger, abuse, pain, greed, selfishness, violence, and war".

Fear is a familiar and insidious force whose strength and effects can only be conquered with gentleness, kindness, compassion, and love. Underneath all unkind acts, from something as subtle as Sister's thoughtless pull on my sleeve, to overt cruelty and brutality, there lies a simple truth. The child that lives inside is scared. How do we know? Because fear is the opposite of love, the absence of trust, the paralysis of tenderness, the reason for all dysfunctional behaviors, the fact beneath anger. Fear is the clenching of your gut and the rise of a gripping sensation that seems to hold you captive to its hypnotic powers. Fear's physiological intention is to alert us to danger, to have us move quickly and instantly to safety. We have evolved into a species that has moved fear out of our bellies and in to our hearts. It's time for this mistake to be corrected.

All religions and spiritual paths challenge us to live in a place of inner reflection and growth, a place of suspended thought and suspended ego. In this place of higher consciousness, we focus on love in order to live, more easily, as loving, compassionate, and kind. The leaders, masters, speakers, and writers who remind us to focus on love might all wear different clothes and read from different sacred texts. But what matters is that we hear their message of love. We listen, we bow our heads, we ask for guidance. We forgive the past and focus on the love that will heal all hearts. This is the one path we all must take. The path of love.

Kindness And Compassion

Many years ago, a friend of mind told me about a mythical forest story that she was formulating in her mind. In her story, there was a special forest of large, loving trees in a secluded place where people could go to be comforted during times of grief. She called it "The Forest Of I Know". In this mythical forest, people in pain, the walking wounded, with their sad hearts pounding, would enter a tree-lined path. In graphic, dramatic detail, they would shout out their angst into the wilderness. Calling out: "I'm hurt! I've been betrayed! Abandoned! I'm in pain and it hurts, it hurts so bad!" The trees would softly sway, tenderly brushing the skin of the crier, comforting, nurturing, and whispering: "I know, I know".

I was telling the story of the forest to another friend, just recently. She was sadly pushing through her own grief as it related to a painful break-up. She told me that she thought The Forest Of I Know was not a mythical place, but a real place, the place of friendship that we find in each other, the place we vulnerably enter when we need to hear the understanding "I know, I know" of another.

There are times, though, when our cries fall on to deaf, defensive, or reluctant ears. This is usually the case during an argument between close intimates. I saw this happen at a dinner gathering I attended not long ago. I sat and watched as a couple's dirty laundry was piled high on the dinner table. As each piece was presented, I knew that I was a witness to the kind of banter we've all participated in, in some way or another, when we felt unloved or unworthy, or any of the other "un's. When we wanted nothing more than to be seen and heard and understood.

During this particular and peculiar dinner experience, one of the many things I thought about was the fact that a prayer for peace had been said before dinner. This especially concerned me because I was the one who said grace. I said a prayer for peace and gratitude before we began our delicious meal but then, the couple's heated argument began before dessert was served. I remembered, then, something I'd read by a Buddhist teacher who said that, if you want peace in your heart, you have to first take a good look at all that is not peaceful in your heart.

Maybe, without the threat of exposure, we don't stop to look deeply at our own way of being. Maybe the exposed peacelessness shines a light on the darker places, the dysfunctional patterns, the disruptive behaviors that we ourselves engage in. As difficult as it may be, we have no choice but to look, once the contents of our dirty laundry have been exposed. What we see and what we learn is that we need to destroy our own disruptive patterns so that we can stop trying to destroy each other. In real war, as in the little wars within ourselves and others, we only want to win. We forget that we cannot create peace with aggression. Aggression begets aggression. With aggression, hearts harden. With kindness, hearts soften. With kindness, we look to each other with compassion, we tend to each other's wounds with tender messages of "I know". And, we don't go to war.

We go to kindness. We go to peace.

Teachers, Preachers

Just recently, a group of friends were talking about elementary school teachers that they remembered fondly; people that they considered as having been especially influential to their lives. They remembered special words of wisdom, support, and encouragement. Words of praise, direction, inspiration. I tried to do the same, and strained to think back clearly, but kept coming up blank. As the conversation went on, I could see that I was the only one not speaking up. I wanted to have a special teacher, too. I began to imagine myself on a talk show, with Rosie or Oprah, and having them ask me who my favorite grade-school teacher was. I found myself worried.

Even with my seemingly senseless, self-imposed imaginary pressure, I couldn't come up with an answer. Perhaps my memory fails me. Perhaps I've told too many eccentric nun stories to remember anything other than the more neurotic characterizations. Not only my friends, but the real guests on Rosie and Oprah can remember their teacher's names, the year everything changed because of them, the often tragic twist of life events that took them away while their memory lives on forever. I wanted one of those. Am I the only one who doesn't have one? I moved in my mind, through the years proceeding high school and college, but I just couldn't come up with any teacher-related epiphanies. And to make it even worse, I didn't even have a crush on any of my teachers. In the end, I had to admit that, while my grade-school learning's are most appreciated, my most memorable influences came outside of the school system.

It has been, consistently, people of artistic passion who stir my muse. People who love who they are, where they are, and most importantly, what they do. Writers, musicians, artists, those who express the depth of their being through their chosen mediums. I fall in literary love, time and again, with weavers of words. I listen to NPR interviews with writers and then I want to make them my teachers, my mentors, my friends. I go to readings and ask authors to sign my books, fantasizing a special inscription of great personal value. After a reading in San Francisco, I almost missed my flight home, in order to shake hands with Alice Walker. At another reading, I considered inviting Isabel Allende over for tea, but handed her a fan letter instead. She hasn't gotten back to me, yet.

Also held dear and in great reverence, are pioneers of passionate spiritual vision. Especially, women who gently yet grandly move through the confines of male religious dogma in order to touch the truth of their soul's journeys. These women pave a path that I have only just begun to walk. Sometimes they are writers, as well as visionaries, which makes them all the more appealing to me. These are women I not only want to learn from, know, and emulate; they are women who represent a life I want to live. Growing up in Catholic school, I was not exposed to women teachers who were passionate and direct and bold. The messages, then, were patriarchal, rigid, and religious, not spiritual and enlightening.

My teachers, now, the people who inspire me most, come to me through books and lectures and audio tapes and tv talk shows, in real-life conversations, in gatherings, in meetings, in every day friendships, in memories. I listen and learn and fall in love with their life-saving messages, messages that remind me of who I am. They are those angels who point me towards the divinity within my own self, implore me to know it, honor it, and to see it in others with compassionate eyes. As Mari Evans wrote in *Nightstar*: "I am a wisp of energy, flung from the core of the universe, housed in flesh and bones and blood". As hosts to this "wisp of energy" also known as the soul, we awaken to the realization of our spiritual essence, our opportunity to experience being both human and divine in one existence. As such, we struggle with the confines and the demands of the ego while embarking on the necessary steps of courage, trust, and faith that lead us closer to spiritual enlightenment.

Struggle is also our teacher; our divine, unique, instructor of feminine transformation. From harshness to compassion, from rigidity to fluidity, from despair to ecstasy, from separation to Unity. In her book, *Fire In The Soul*, Joan Borysynko states: "I am given the circumstances I require for my awakening. Every situation, seen rightly, contains the seeds of freedom." In my life, for the most part, women have assisted in planting the seeds for me, for my learning, for my growth. They walk ahead, pointing out the stumbling blocks that I, inevitably, stumble upon. Falling often, getting up every time, I hold on to the truth of their teachings and the truth of my own, eventual, spiritual homecoming.

Friendship

Ascribing a definition to my friendships brings me to a

meaning that I've only just recently come to truly know. From an earlier way of life, when friendship meant sharing secrets and good times, cherished memories of lives and transitions, we grew into women who took friendship a step further, to a place of deeper love, deeper caring, going so far as to even take responsibility for the mutual growth of our individualities, for the growth of the friendships we were nurturing, and for the spiritual paths we are committed to.

Long term friends from my younger years know a part of me, a yesterday me, that continues to be a sampling of who I now am, a me I can see and remember through their eyes, through our shared memories, and through the laughter that fills my home when we look back together. My newer friends, the friends of the current me, don't share as long a history, but they do share a new knowing, an understanding of who I am now, who I've become, as a result of who I once was. Together, we look towards a tomorrow that will be painted, together, with new brushes, new colors, new scenes. In a relatively short period of time, we've reached an understanding, a commitment to our family-like bond, that came from this coming together at a time of spiritual intent. We are sisters, spiritual sisters, linked to each other's hearts by way of our soul's journeys.

Spiritual sisters find each other, as travelers tend to find their own in foreign countries. We speak the same language, a language of dedication to a path that holds nothing more than the promise of more. More knowing, more love, more compassion, more kindness, more awakening to spiritual truths. Spiritual sisterhood is something more than friendship. It is something that bonds us heart to heart, and beyond our hearts, to our soul's purpose. The mystical and mysterious energy that brought us together is not unlike the energy of attraction that brings lovers together in a joining of dedicated lives. The soul connection of friendship is just as powerful, just as meaningful, and just as enticing.

Recently, at my kitchen table, we came together, a few of my spiritual sisters and I. We had transformed ourselves into a Board of Directors for the Interfaith Church and Spiritual Community Center we dream of creating. We call it: Interfaith Alliance Ministries (IAM). We had come so far in a short period of time and yet it was as if we had always known each other, or we had always known that we would find each other, find ourselves in this shared moment of creation. In our lives we often encounter a nagging knowing that hangs onto our growing up, our ins and outs of the journey's road, the road that brings us to a moment in time when we can finally say "ah yes, here it is, here is the place I've been looking for, the place where I can stop and take my rest. The place where my dreams are welcome." That place is in the heart of a loving friend, a spiritual sister. And that is where we found ourselves.

A group of women sitting at the table. We started out as friends often do; sharing stories, trading secrets, and listening to what was between the lines. We all crashed and splattered at similar times and for similar reasons, each of us helping the other pick up broken pieces. But this time, unlike other times in our lives, we helped each other to put the pieces back differently. We helped each other to discard the unnecessary ways. We held each other throughout the purgings, the breakdowns, and the resurrections. Together, we dreamed of more meaningful lives, lives that would somehow survive the destruction of our fantasies. We held on to the belief in an inner sanctity, a healing that would come from our prayers to whomever and whatever might be listening. We drew pictures, wrote stories, read books, burned little pieces of paper on full moon nights. We watched each other grow stronger. We compared our paths and found them to be one.

Together, we woke up to a spiritually focused life. Together we watch out for each other as we see the world differently. We are no longer willing to participate as slaves to unhealthy patterns, while understanding that we had to release the perceived benefits of holding on to our old wounds. Our wounds were the hooks we previously used as ways to bond with others. We encouraged each other to replace the mindset of victim-hood with a strength of conviction that gave way to a more courageous way of being. Together, we found unconditional respect within our friendships, a level of caring once considered unattainable. Spiritual sisters share a love that looks both ways; from the past to the future, in order to assist, encourage, and escort our loved ones toward their highest good. Spiritual sisters are more than friends, more than family. We are lovers of each other's souls.

It is not to say, in looking at a spiritual sister/friendship, that we don't giggle like girls, or playfully move through each other's lives, as all good friends do. We go to the movies, go dancing, talk about our love lives, laugh at who we used to be, and often at who we are. We cry for each other misfortunes and heartaches, we cheer and celebrate each other's victories. We promise not to be friends with each others ex's, and we keep each other informed on favorite TV shows that one or the other might miss. But, more than this, more than what we've always known friendship to be, we hold each other up to the light of spirit, to the light of blessings, of renewal, of growth. We hold each other in our hearts of prayer.

On the day I graduated from the Seminary, I looked over my shoulder to see a row of spiritual sisters in attendance. Some had flown from Florida to New York. Some were friends from the area who took the Staten Island Ferry, with children in tow. Others were friends who took time away from their busy lives, who walked into a church they'd never seen, in order to support me, to praise me, to let me know that they believed in me. And for those who could not be there, a party way thrown to let me know that my path, the one that I was determined to pave, was the one that they would walk with me.

Months later, when I called that meeting of the Board of Directors, to begin the mission of the Interfaith church, some of the women sitting there with me were those who never stopped believing in my dream and who never once shied away from admitting that this was their dream, too. Spiritual sisters share a dream of endless magnitude, a dream of spiritual living, a dream of kindness, compassion, and camaraderie. The Vietnamese Zen Buddhist Monk, Ticht Nacht Hahn, in his lecture on love, says that the most blessed and meaningful thing that you can say to a loved one is: "I am here for you". This is what is said in the friendships of spiritual sisters. This is what is proven in the easy interactions of friendships that are committed to loving-kindness, spiritual values, and mutual support.

I am a lucky woman. I am blessed beyond my limited understanding of what the universe has to offer. My life is filled with spiritual sisters, friendships that fill my world with their caring, their availability, their assistance, words of wisdom, generosity. My friends are my sisters, my teachers, my heart, and my soul. My life is touched and enhanced because of the blessing of their presence.

Heroes

At a recent writing circle meeting, the group members decided to write a descriptive narrative about the things we noticed around the room we were writing in. The woman to my right made reference to the bracelet I was wearing and referred to it as "ever present". Later, we wrote about people who were most influential in our lives. At that point, my writing took a step back and told the story of abuelita's bracelet.

During the Christmas holidays of the year I turned 16, I decided to make and spend my own money for gifts. I worked a few hours a week at a kiosk in the Woodbridge Center Mall doing minor jewelry repair, I baby-sat the kids down the street, and I sold my Yamaha guitar. Two weeks before Christmas, I counted my earnings. I thought I had enough money for everyone on my list, but ran out before I could make a purchase for my abuelita (grandmother). Having left my favorite family member for last left me with empty pockets and a panic. I paced, stressed, sweat, cried, and anguished over what to do for her. Finally, I decided that I would just make her something while at work in the mall. Since all I had on hand there were little clips, clasps, hooks, and repair tools, I had to get creative. I disassembled a thick silver chain from my mother's umbrella , took it with me to my job, and created a heavy but pretty bracelet for my sweet and special recipient.

My abuelita treated her bracelet like an expensive, rare jewel. She put it on, displayed it with great, dramatic expressions of admiration, and swore to never take it off. It wasn't long after those holidays that she began to take ill, complaining of frequent stomach pains and fatigue. I told her that I thought she spent too much time indoors and that I would be taking her on rides out to the beach once I turned 17 and got my license to drive. Since my birthday is five days before Christmas, I planned on an extraordinary holiday excursion just for the purpose of improving her health. She said she liked the idea, even as she lay in bed looking out into a distance that I couldn't see.

In early December of the year I was to turn 17, my grandmother was taken to the hospital for some routine tests. Within hours of her admission, she was transferred to the intensive care unit. I watched from across the large ward-like room as too many tubes were inserted into her frail arms and as she strained against all the poking and prodding. Usually most kind and accommodating, she loudly reprimanded a nurse for what I assumed was a painful procedure. But no, the nurse told me later, she was upset because someone tried to take off her bracelet.

I had one visit at my abuelita's bedside. We had a brief, loving chat before I was ushered out and told to wait until the next visiting period. In those days, visitors were only allowed in the ICU once every two hours. As I waited for time to pass in the waiting room, I stared down at the floor and ignored the conversations of family and friends, resenting the fact that they, too, would want time with her. When the designated amount of time passed, I got up and took my place at the ICU door, determined to be the first in line. I peeked in and noticed that she was too quiet and still. I went back to the waiting room and told my mother that something was wrong. She got up to investigate. When she came back, she sat across from me, took my hand, and handed me my abuelita's bracelet. I put it on and swore, silently, that I would never take it off.

Almost 30 years have passed since I made that promise

to my grandmother's spirit while kneeling in a dark New Jersey hospital chapel. Needless to say, I've been through several altered versions of that first makeshift bracelet. But, there's always one on my wrist, every day, every year, even after all these years.

It wouldn't be entirely true to say that I feel as though I always have her near me or that the rite of wearing the bracelet is always done with her in mind. But her mark was made as an influence that has remained with me. In the telling of the story, I remembered her as my first hero.

My heroes have always been those closest to me. One such hero is a friend who makes me muffins and salads. Another reads whatever I write with the knowing of a long-time reader. One comes out of her shell every now and then to talk to me about her heart. I have a hero who longs to shield me from harm, several who travel far to come visit me, to celebrate my every milestone. I have a hero who sends me feathers from another world. I have heroes who share their wisdom, their homes, their love, their kindness, their families, their lives. How much more they matter to me than the bigger names, the people who would have us call them by titles or recognition of achievement. My heroes have titles that don't get put on business cards. Good Friend, Kind Helper, Compassionate Soul. My heroes come in to my heart and stay. Perhaps my abuelita's bracelet represents each one of them. Perhaps it's a well-worn remainder of my very many blessings. Abuelita's bracelet carries life and love and memories. I'll never take it off.

Loving

Thanks to a seemingly unquenchable thirst for an understanding of the human heart, mind, and spirituality, I have become an avid reader of psychological case studies, self-help books, new thought philosophies, and theories of spiritual perspectives. I am consistently amazed, impressed, and often touched, by stories that allow me to look deeper into realms of wisdom as they pertain to our mysterious ways of being. And yet, regardless of my interest in theories and/or the theorists, sometimes it is a taste of good old-fashioned fiction that gives me the greatest inspiration and insight. For example, in her book, *The Way Forward Is With A Broken Heart*, Alice Walker creates a scenario for us to peek in on the marriage of a young couple during an evening's conversation. The female character in the story has fallen in love with another man. She tells her husband about the attraction and of her intense desire for him. She tells her husband the things she both likes and dislikes about this man, whom she works with, on a daily basis. Her husband listens to her, comforts her when she expresses her angst, then he pours her a bath.

Now, there's more to the story, but I was struck by a line where the husband thinks about how to handle his wife's desire for another man and he decides that the most important thing for him to do is to love her back into his heart. He doesn't try to control or manipulate or guilt her back. He just loves her. Now, thanks to Alice Walker's flair for perfect prose, I was able to over-look the improbable fact that the hero was a man who seemed just too good to be true. But the point was made that there is something about the purity of what love is, in its originally intended ego-less form, as opposed to what we, in our pridefulness want it to be, that makes no judgment and creates no posturing for self-gratification.

This is not to suggest that any of us could easily listen and accept a lover's expressed desire, love, or obsession for another person. But it is to say that there is a quality to the truth of love's essence that should allow for someone we love to be true to him or herself, regardless of where that leaves us. As complex as we are as individuals, the dynamics of who we are and how we are in intimate relationships takes us to a level of complexity that often leaves us baffled, confused, and hopefully, amused. When a lover looks away, there are a number of psychological factors that can be referenced. Childhood issues, family patterns, intimacy problems, poor communication in the relationship, whatever. We know all that. We've heard all that. What we want to find is a way to cut through all the confusion and the complexity so that we can go back to having our lives simple, easy, comfortable, and secure.

But, beyond the valid and often necessary process of couple's counseling and/or individual therapy, the real work is in acknowledging that there is a soul's purpose for every relationship. In the good, the bad, the difficult, and the joyful, our relationships are opportunities to look into a mirror of our own soulful-ness, to see the reflection of a divine force that is sacred and powerful and beyond any possible coincidence. The "old" lover looked for someone who would take care of her, fulfill her desire for completeness, for having old wounds healed, new wounds licked. She wanted someone she could mold and manipulate to fit her ideals and needs. She engaged in power struggles and conflict. She suffered and felt empty, even when in an intimate relationship. She repeated patterns, hoping that the next person would understand her better, love her inner child, her outer child, her PMS. She went to therapy and learned about active listening and "I statements". And then she fell into what she believed to be love and, again, expected her lover to make up for all the wrongs of her past.

The truly loving lover looks for a spiritual partner, a love that is based on a mutual dedication to the soul growth of the other person. The loving lover understands the complexity of the human spirit and the importance of honoring the differences between two people. The eyes, the voice, the life of her beloved are understood to be arrows pointing to her own path. The mysterious force that brought you together is the force that touches your heart, that gives you an opportunity to suspend your ego, not just when in the ecstasy, but also when in the mundane. The creation of a spiritual relationship is the loving lover's goal. The loving lover sees that the old way didn't work because it was based on a union of egos. A spiritual approach longs, instead, for a union of souls, one that teaches you how to listen, and see with your heart.

Relating to a beloved with an emphasis on mutual spiritual growth doesn't take away from the frivolous, the fun or the erotic aspects of the relationship. In fact, it can enhance the relationship on all levels because the emphasis is on accepting the other person, honoring who they are as they are. This gift of love bridges gaps in understanding because the lines of communication are padded with safety and acceptance. What is seen in the other is the sacredness of their very existence. Concentrating on the sacred makes loving each other magical.

Ah, but inevitably, there are times when we see something about them that we find unpleasant. What then? We have to remind ourselves that our romance is our mirror. We have to do the hard work of rigorous introspection before we speak in harsh judgment. In her book: *The Path Of Transformation*, Shakti Gawain tells us: "Along with letting the other person know our feelings, including ways we might wish they would change, we need to remind ourselves that we brought them into our lives to teach and inspire us to develop new aspects of ourselves." And in his book, *The Quiet Answer*, Hugh Prather says: "If we are ever to know love without limits, there can be no range to our giving. To want something from another person is to utterly misunderstand their role in our happiness".

And so, the challenge for the spiritually loving lover is to be gentle and kind and accepting and compassionate, even when it threatens the ego's pride. She allows herself to be stretched, extended, and enhanced by participating in a shared experience of fearless giving. She prays for her beloved's well-being and she opens her heart to the possibility of either forever or not. In making a commitment to a love life based on spiritual principles, the foundation is set for trust, truth, compassion, passion, and friendship.

Home

Not a commonly used Spanish word, querencia is literally defined as "fondness, affection, and yearning". The New World translation dictionary further defines it as "nest". As it is used, the word describes a feeling of being home. In her book, *Writing Towards Home*, Georgia Heard says that querencia is "a place where one feels safe, a place from which one's strength of character is drawn. Our bodies know where we feel most a home. Our bodies will tell us, if we will listen." Our bodies tell us when we have found home. Our hearts tell us. We are happiest when our body and heart finds peaceful rest. As life changes and moves all around and through us, we can either flow with the movement or resist. Understandably, we want to hold on to our comforts. We want to hold on to that which makes us feel at home, that which makes us feel querencia.

In discussing this concept with friends, the theme kept returning to love-lives; first loves, places visited with lovers, homes shared, homes broken. Querencia cannot be separated from the undeniable blissful state of being in love. And so, in the interest of querencia's romantic implication, I remember my first true love, and the bug bite that took me to querencia.

I'd been lying out by my pool when I got bit by a bug. I don't know what kind of bug it was because I never saw it. All I had as evidence were the tiny little dots it left as its mark on my skin. I didn't think much of it at the time, I just put a dab of greasy stuff that a good friend swore was a miracle cream. The next day, the dots had multiplied into little separate neighborhoods of alien conglomerations across my back. They looked like prickly intruders that were going to take over my skin for their new home and they were inviting all their friends and relatives to join them. My new love, my beloved, went to the health food store and bought some Aztec Indian clay to draw out the bug poison, but it was too late.

Three days passed, and I had become very ill. My head was pounding with a severe headache, my stomach was continuously nauscous, and I was extremely fatigued. In and out of fevers, I would open my eyes to my beloved, tending to my bug-poisoning. Slowly, I recuperated by way of allergy medicine, chocolate ice cream, and loving care. As my physical ailments healed, my heart began to soar. A mysterious, un-necessary insect had caused me much distress. But then, there was the love bug. Corny, yes. But true. I had been bitten by that as well. As my physical health returned, my heart expanded with an affection that felt as though I could understand, for the first time in my life, the creation of dreams for a lifetime. I had found a place of familiar comfort. I had found querencia.

Querencia changes, as do all things in life. Often, it is only for a moment that we can hold on to a person, a place, or a situation that takes us to the depth of our hearts. It is in those moments that we take our deepest breath. When changes do occur, they are often painful because they take the home out of our hearts and leave us feeling homeless. We feel as though we've lost our way, as children do when they release a holding hand and begin to journey out on their own. A frightening time of change, growth, and opportunity. Luckily, querencia does not run out. It only changes form.

W. Somerset Maugham, in "The Moon and Sixpence", written in 1919, wrote the following: "Sometimes a person hits upon a place to which he mysteriously feels that he belongs. Here is the home he sought, and here he will settle amid scenes that he has never seen before, among people he has never known, as though they were familiar to him from her birth. Here, at last, he finds rest."

Chapter 5

The Spiritual Path

Unity

B efore I decided to become a minister, there were a lot of things that I was sure were right about how I viewed the world. I had been told early in life that I was made in the image and likeness of God. And then I was told that God was loving but angry, kind but judgmental, unconditional but in need of praise. I wanted be just like God. And so, when I was angry I expressed it with self-righteousness. When I was judgmental, I knew I was right. And when I was ego-laden with the need for recognition, I felt justified.

To me, looking in the mirror meant defining a product. Who I saw in there needed to have achieved a certain amount of professional notoriety, a specific degree of academics, and a particularly special kind of lover, one who complimented all that was good and wonderful about me.

After I began the seminary, everything changed. Suddenly, I was faced with a novel concept. That being the possibility of my having been wrong. A lot. About a lot of things. Mostly, I was wrong about thinking that my own individual ego was real and important. I was wrong to think that I am separate from others, simply because my physical body is different and apart. The concept of one mind, one love, one consciousness was, and continues to be, an evolution of learning and understanding.

Marianne Williamson, in a lecture on The Course In Miracles, warns that once you make a commitment to living a spiritually dedicated life, God sends in a wrecking ball to aid in the reconstruction of your belief system. My prideful ways met their semi-destruction with a lot of noise, pain, resistance, and selfish negotiations. Well, as it turns out, there is no negotiating with Divine Truth. On the path to living a life concentrated in peace and love, you have to look at all that is not loving and peaceful within yourself. Sad to say, it's often not such a pretty picture, but one that must be gently acknowledged and embraced. It is only by living with and moving through your shadow's image, can you see the light of your true self. Your true self, the self that is and of God, is one that lives deep beneath the ego's strength. It is accessible. It is yours.

I remember, clearly, watching the news a few weeks after the 9-11 terrorists attacks. Osama Bin Laden was making statements of war against the United States. He was saying that we, Americans, had declared war on Islam and that we are sinners. As he spoke, I watched him and tried not to focus on the holy war that seemed to be brewing within my own self. "Child of God", I said to his video-taped eyes. How very difficult it was, in those moments to sustain my commitment to see all people as children of God, as parts of my own self, as elements of my own consciousness, as my brothers. And yet, what are my choices? I addressed the television again: "You are a child of God, Osama Bin Laden. Child of God, we pray for the correction of your mind and heart".

Opportunities to think in terms of peace, love, and unity present themselves in a world of mirrors, reflections of ourselves as seen through our intimate relationships, our interactions with strangers and yes, even through our angst and judgments of terrorists. Negative thoughts we harbor towards any individual or group are thoughts that come back to show themselves to us in some form of karmic reality. When we raise our voices or our attitudes of self righteous indignation in an attempt to declare what another has done wrong, we need to, then, take a moment to turn toward the mirror. We need to say a prayer for the child we see there. And we need to pray for the child we have judged as angry or jealous or bitter or cruel. The prayer of St. Francis asks that we be made "An instrument of peace". In so asking, we must recognize our own peacelessness. In so doing, we come closer to being peaceful.

I recently heard a woman speak of her spiritual path. Like me, she had researched and searched all of the major world religions, she attended retreats, lived in ashrams, took classes on self-transformation. She looked everywhere for God, look for answers, for direction. What she found was that God was not out in the wilderness of the world waiting for her to find him/her/it. God was within her, deeply shrouded and covered by her own resistance to truly touch the depth of her own image and likeness of God.

At a recent peace/prayer vigil, I asked those in attendance to maintain a consciousness of peace in the face of our country's experience with terrorist attacks. We read peace prayers from around the world, words from Islam, Christianity, Judaism, Wiccan, American Indian, African, and New Thought. Not surprisingly, they each in their own way, called for the understanding that "Peace begins with me." It is up to each individual to make a commitment to focus on peace. We can collectively contribute to a miraculous shift away from a consciousness of war and hatred. The work that needs to be done is a constant discipline, long and arduous, painful and painstaking. But, if it were easy, we would not know the extent of our own potential. Light will be provided and illuminating grace will make the path's direction clear.

Surviving The Bumpy Road

There is a Buddhist story about a spiritual awakening that starts with a madman on the warpath. The madman was known for his particular vicious anger towards sages and siddhas. He would go from village to village chopping off the heads of the wisest and most respected wise men and women. One day, while walking through a crowd that feared him, he came upon a monk nun peacefully sleeping while leaning against a Bodhi Tree. He hovered over her with a menacing look and waited for her to look up at him. When she did, he pulled out a sword and held it over her head. "What do you want from me?" she asked him. "I want you to take me to the path of peace" he told her, while secretly knowing that she would be like all the rest, all those who tried but could not help him to find the peace he inwardly longed for. The monk closed her eyes and took a long, deep breath. "You are a mean and ugly man" she said. "All that you practice is power, control, and the care of your angry, unkind ego. Why should I talk to you of peace, if you are unwilling to be peaceful?" With rage in his belly, the madman pulled back his sword and aimed for the woman's throat. With compassion in her eyes she looked up at him and said "You see, there is the reason you do not know peace. You live in the hell of your own madness". Humbled, the madman lowered his head. Relieved, he threw down his sword. "And now" said the woman "You know the path to peace".

So often, we go through our daily lives as that madman, with our swords held out in fear and angst and anger while truly yearning for peace and love. We find it difficult to step out from behind the armor of our defenses. We find it difficult to throw down our swords in order to trust the way of loving- kindness, for fear that we will be let down, abandoned. We try to find balance between our soul's journey, which emphasizes peaceful living, and our ego's pride, which looks out defensively and fearfully, for any signs of danger. What we often fail to realize is that our experiences of conflict are often no more than erroneous perceptions. To find peace, to find the path to peace, we need only begin with one step inward. In a poem by the Sufi poet, Rumi, he tells us: "I have lived on the lip of insanity, wanting to know reason. I knock on a door. It opens. I've been knocking from the inside." There is no need to go outside. The path to peace begins with an inward journey.

In the Course In Miracles, we are taught that there are only two emotions; love and fear. The ego functions from a

81

place of fear and lives defensively, mistakenly believing in the power of others to hurt us. It retaliates by taking on a defensive stance of its own, to protect itself from the possibility of harm. On the other hand, love sees everything from a perspective of compassion and non-judgment. Errors previously considered as "sins" in need of punishment are understood to be mistakes in need of corrections. We often recognize both fear and love as factors that motivate us on a daily basis. The challenge is to struggle against fear, the ego's pride, so that love prevails and dominates our being. In so doing, we can live peacefully without any swords to weigh us down. The show-down between fear and love often finds itself deeply rooted in what is known as the Dark Night. The Dark Night is a time of devastating and painful transition, ultimately ending in an overall humbling and a renewal of the soul. The Dark Night of the soul experience is like trying to survive the Australian Outback, except that, instead of the outdoor elements, we are pitted against the self-defeating elements of the ego.

Imagine being alone and stranded with nothing more than the characteristics of ego. In a world filled with magical and mystical wonders, the ego sees obstacles and turmoil. The ego is scared, easily angered, judgmental, oriented towards material gain. Recently, while talking with a friend about an erroneous judgment I'd made about someone, I told her that I wish I could bite out the part of my brain that made harsh and quick judgments against people. How can I do that without brain surgery? What tools do I need in order to be more like the peaceful monk and less like the sword-wielding madman?

The ego gives us temporary jolts of energy. We are momentarily enthralled by our sense of power and control.

But true and lasting joy comes from having our lives touched by the wonders of God and nature that are repeatedly given to us day after day. It is never boring, never anything less than awe-inspiring to experience God's sunrise, God's sunset, God's gift of a friendship, a lover, all of which leave you breathless and grateful and joyful. Perhaps, then, all that is needed to tame the ego is the constant renewal of perception. A moment taken to detach from an unkind judgment as it is forming. A walk taken to release fear or anger or angst to the beauty of the ocean, the park, the beautiful new morning. A kiss and a hug from a child to remind us of our own innocence and the innocence of all others, all our brothers and sisters who join us on our path to peace.

We need to learn how to live from the truth of our being, not from the lie of our ego's influence. To do this, we need to be willing to see ourselves and each other with loving eyes, eyes of compassion. We need to adhere to a sense of kindness and acceptance that acknowledges without judgment, the good and the bad, the old and the new, the child and the adult within each person, their shadow as well as their light. The key element, the most essential tool in this awakening to spiritual survival, is love. Love is ultimately, all that matters, all that is. The opposite of fear, the reason for heart beats, the reason for breath. Love is the driving force behind our very existence. Everything else, every other thing, is ego/pride/fear. What we know in our hearts, is that only love is real.

When we all live as spiritual survivors, from a place of love, on a path of peace, we will live as it was written in *The Prophet*, by Kahil Gibran: "Awake at dawn with a winged heart and give thanks for another day of loving. Rest at noon and meditate on love's ecstasy. Return home at evening's tide with gratitude. Sleep with a prayer for the beloved in your heart, and a song of praise upon your lips."

Signs

"And the sign said long hair-ed, freaky people need not apply". That's how the song started, one that I played on my guitar, many many years ago with the few chords I knew then (the only chords I know to this day). It was a song about signs that tell us to "do this don't do that". The singer expressed feeling overwhelmed by all the negative implications in the signs he was reading (classist, racist, sexist messages), until he came upon the one that said "everybody welcome to come in, kneel down and pray".

When I played that song on my guitar and loudly sang out the words, I was thinking in terms of literal signs, signs written in black and white, big bold messages to those of us who were, at that time, the younger generation. We were the generation that chanted "drugs, sex, rock and roll" 20 years before we made TV commercials telling our own children to just say no. We rebelled against the signs and we revolutionized the times. It was a great time to be young.

Years later, I came to understand that not all signs were as literal as the billboards of my youth. I had to learn the art of tuning in to the subtleties of nature and synchronicity. The first person to bring ethereal signs to my attention was my friend Cecilia. A spiritual guide dressed in practical every day-ness and a Mexican accent, she faithfully followed her intuition and the signs that drew her inward. She helped me to break out of my insistent analytical, left-brain thinking so that my inner eye had fewer obstacles through which to truly view the buena vista that has turned out to be my life.

Once, while driving together through the highways of Mexican mountains, I noticed signs posted all along the dangerously driven roads that said "Respeta Tus Signales" (Respect Yours Signs). When I pointed them out, she laughed and told me that the road signs were sending a much greater message than that of traffic control. Cecilia would watch the day's activities, people passing, events unfolding and she could find meaningful messages in most anything. Eventually, I came to believe, as she did, that signs are everywhere, pointing us in specific directions, advising us on what to do and sometimes, simply, to remind us that we are not alone. I'd note the subtle sign of a little bird landing within my sight during a moment of sadness or a more stirring flash of insight while staring out into the nothingness of an early morning's mediation. I hear differently now, so that I don't miss the whisper of God's voice, which comes to me through the wisdom of strangers and friends, suddenly my gurus, even if only for a moment.

When my good friend Miah was dying, a few years ago, I began to find bird feathers in strange places. At the time, we lived several states away from each other and planned on my going to see her for a visit. While she was recovering from an operation, I felt strongly that I needed to go soon, but she asked me to wait until she felt stronger. That's when the feathers began to appear. I would walk to my car and find a feather under the tire. I went to the gym and found a feather stuck to the hinge of the door. I even found feathers in my home, as if blown in by the wind.

Feathers were everywhere, compelling me to pick them up and save them until I had a big bowl full in my living room. One night, I dreamt that I was walking up a hill and saw Miah up ahead of me by a few hundred yards. I ran to catch up to her and called out her name. When she turned around to look at me I held out my bowl of feathers to show her. She smiled at me and held up a dead eagle that she was carrying, upside down, by the legs. She said, "I have a lot of feathers too!" Her smile was loving and kind, as she always was. The dream changed to the two of us in her kitchen. She hugged me and told me that I could always count on her.

As Miah's illness progressed, I was told about an Indian healer who went to visit her on her deathbed. By way of ceremonial release, he opened a bag of earth-medicine, which included hundreds of feathers. The feathers were scattered all around her bed. I knew, then, that I would never see her alive again.

After Miah's death, I went to her memorial service with my feathers packed in my carry-on bag. If I listed all the signs that were presented to me while I was on my way to her memorial with my feathers, this story would begin to sound like science fiction. Suffice to say, that the signs were everywhere there, telling me of her presence, of god's presence, of a language that lives in our world that is from another world and that speaks to us, clearly, when we have the willingness to see and hear. On a very dark night, I walked out to my car after the memorial service. I scattered feathers along my path. When I got in my rental car, I began to cry and I cried for a very long time. Driving through unfamiliar streets, I looked over to my empty passenger seat and I spoke to Miah as if she were there with me. Then I turned on the radio and a song was playing that sealed in my belief in signs, forever. From the soundtrack of the movie *Waiting To Exhale*, Whitney Houston and Cece Winans were singing: "Count On Me", a song about forever friendship.

That song from the 70's about signs ends with the line: "Thank you, Lord for thinking 'bout me. I'm alive and doing fine." Yes, thank you, Lord. I'm alive and doing fine. Thank you for the signs.

Commitment

Every year, for many years, I would make a New year's Resolution to live a more spiritual life, to be nicer, kinder, more disciplined, more compassionate. But year after year, at each year's end, I'd look back and see that I had failed. I'd scratch my head and wonder why I couldn't seem to get out of my own way so that I could do what I really believed was the right way to live. My biggest mistake, I can see now, was to take my commitment lightly. I did not take the time to make a daily re-commitment to the changes that were necessary in order for me to truly connect with God. Forging a personal path to the spiritual life is each soul's ultimate, individual plan. It is just a matter of when we realize it , acknowledge it, and figure out how we want to go about it. Each and every major religion can give you a hint as to how they believe you can do it, and all the new thought philosophers have books you can read that gives you some guidelines. Everyone is right, to some degree. Here are some things to consider:

Mindfulness: This was a tough one, initially. I'd been so caught up in who I was, what I had, where I'd been, and where I was going, that I almost didn't get to see what was right there in front of me at any given moment. Living in the moment is a mindfulness task. The Buddhists refer to it as chopping wood and carrying water. It's about allowing yourself to be in each and every moment. Even the most mundane of tasks carry the potential for great joy and wonder. Look, listen, breathe, feel, smell. No matter what it is, no matter what you are doing. Pay attention to your intentions. Take responsibility for the consequences of your behavior, your words and even your thoughts. Being mindful allows you to truly experience the truth of who you and the experience of every moment.

Kindness: We would all like to think of ourselves as nice people. But what happens when our buttons get pushed and our defenses kick in? Kindness is an attribute that allows for us to take a step away from anger or pride in order to better understand the situation from all perspectives. It has often been said that that our greatest adversaries are also our greatest teacher. Mother Teresa was known for referring to her greatest challenges as "Jesus in his many distressing disguises". Kindness allows us to see the guru, the teacher, the master, the friend, the soul, the child of God behind every difficult person. Perhaps, as we cultivate kindness to its ultimate perfection, we will even be able to see ourselves in them. And then , we will finally see perfection.

Honesty: Honesty is a rigorous chore. It's not just about saying the right thing, the kind of thing that would hold up as true in a court of law. It's about being truthful to the very core of your being, knowing what the truth is for you in any given situation and at any given time. In order to be rigorously honest, you must be willing to face the areas of yourself and your life that might need to be changed. Rigorous honesty is about not lying to yourself. You always know what's true. Even if you have to look deeply to find the truth, look deeply. It will, indeed, set you free.

Forgiveness: This one is all about looking in the mirror. Forgiveness is such a big and important step that you have to know that you are ready and willing to give up any of the comforts that come with the package of victim-hood. If you truly enjoy being upset with someone and you like all the attention that it has gotten you, then you're not ready. Forgiveness is about caring enough to clean out the dirty drawer of the past. Forgiving, forgetting, a n d letting go is not about finding and saying the right prayer, it's about saying the same prayer over and over and over again until you pray yourself in to a peaceful, loving heart. Every thought you think goes in to the universal prayer log and comes back to you as a reality for you to live. So pay attention to what you are thinking. Your thoughts are prayers. Think thoughts and pray prayers of forgiveness and peace and kindness and love. With this, you will find your heaven.

Pray: In her book, *Traveling Mercies*, Anne Lamont says that she only prays two prayers. One is: "Help! help! Help!" and the other is: "thank you! thank you! thank you!" Perhaps that is all it has to be. Make up your own prayers, whatever feels right for you. But pray. Pray all the time. Something is happening when you pray, something wonderful and focused and promising and perfect. But remember to watch your thoughts, be careful with where

you put your mind. Your thoughts are prayers, remind
yourself. Prayer is not a formal set of pre-recorded
sentences, but a state of mind, a way of being. Pray. Be
prayerful.

Awe: Take time to feel grateful, because every moment
holds the promise of great wonders. Life can be, for you,
as it is told in a poem by William Blake: "See the world in
a grain of sand. See heaven in a wild flower. Hold infinity
in the palm of your hand. Hold eternity in an hour". Be in
awe. And, be grateful.

Chapter 6

Peace

Religious Pluralism

E very year, when the chill of December comes
around, I long to return home to New York for the
Christmas holidays. As a little girl, I would walk in
wonderland through the light-streamed streets and rejoice
in the celebration that seemed to life everyone's spirits.
The smell of roasted peanuts filled the air and Christmas
Carols greeted shoppers at every department store doorway.
I didn't know then , when I was very young, that there were
people who didn't celebrate exactly as my own family did.
We had Latin rhythms mixed in with holiday music,
quantities of rice and beans that could feed the entire town,
and a tree that was saved until Christmas Eve to decorate.

As I got older, I came to see and understand that there
were people who were not Puerto Rican and who weren't
even Catholic. They did things differently, and I was

fascinated. Some didn't eat rice and beans with their holiday meals, which I really didn't understand, but there were so many some interesting and delicious alternative foods that I was discovering and enjoying. Years later, when I began to lean about the different religions and their rites, rituals and celebrations, I came to believe in the concept of religious pluralism, which eventually led me to the path of Interfaith.

The concept of religious pluralism is based on the theory that dogmatic religion is culturally-based, while simultaneously being universal in it spiritual principles. Studies of religious events and texts/scriptures allow for the probability of a divine inervention/communication/contact as having occurred in different continents during one particular period of time (1500 BC/BCE to the beginning of the first millennium). People formulated interpretations of that communication based on their specific cultural perspectives. They were all getting the message, the direction, and the encouragement to transcend the human ego in favor of a higher spiritual consciousness. But, the culture, language, climate, and historical circumstances created philosophical differences alone with different partial applications of the same divine message.

Here in the United States, we see people who had their religious upbringing in Christianity who celebrate Kwanzaa in honor of their African roots. People who began in the Jewish religion who are now practicing Buddhism or who celebrate Winter Solstice because they now adhere to the earth- bound or Wiccan philosophies. We hear of the Islamic Ramadan, the Hindu Divali, Hanukah and Christmas. We are blessed to live in a country that celebrates religious freedom, so that we can investigate, convert, celebrate, or just peek in at any and all that the different religions have to offer.

People everywhere, throughout the year, celebrate something in the same of their religion. We commemorate birth, new birth, re-birth, virgin birth, death, marriage, the earth, trees, suns, moon, harvest, rain, gods , goddesses, rain, babies, miracles. We play special music, sit in silence, light candles, dance, pray, chant, exchange gifts. But when the winter holidays arrive, we see most clearly where culture and history most dramatically influence our spiritual practices. We tend to go back to our roots.

With a most respectful, humble bow to the world faith, religions, and philosophies that inspire me and motivate me, I am taken back to my own roots during the American Christmas holidays. Even while living in the no-snow sunshine of southern Florida, I can easily be transported, by way of my heart, to a time of snowmen, salvation army santas, and breath that can be seen as smoke when I speak. Bundled up in a new Christmas coat while sucking on a peppermint candy cane, I hum along to " Oh, Come let us adore him.", while getting misty-eyed and thinking: "Oh, I do, I do!"

On the New York streets of my memory, the winter holidays unify the masses. On the streets of my memory, there is a strategically placed nativity scene that miraculously lifts the spirits of all people. They pause and are touched with a sense of grace, peace, brotherhood, and joy.

Oh, come let us adore each other. Let our hearts be open to all gods, all good, all that is holy and hopeful. Let us move into the next breath with kindness, compassion, gratitude, love, and peace.

World Peace

A few months after my ordination, in June 2000, I received a call from the executive director of The Interfaith Council For Freedom of Worship in Tibet. (This was exactly one year before the terrorist attacks on the United States.) At that time, the concept of religious freedom, vs. religious persecution was not so widely discussed or even recognized. I was asked to participate in the development of a world-wide publication that would bring the plight of the Tibetan people to the American public. What follows is the message I wrote for circulation Internationally. Houses of worship are welcome to use this message in their services when speaking about the importance of religious tolerance and freedom. The service, in its entirety, can still be seen on the internet. While it speaks, specifically, of the Tibetan people, we know that it speaks, also, to all people everywhere who are suppressed, oppressed, tortured, and killed for what they believe in. May peace prevail. The message:

We are here today to acknowledge the existence of religious persecution in Tibet. We are here to acknowledge that there is not one person who can be truly free, until all people are truly free. We are here today for the people of Tibet, to take the suffering of our Tibetan brothers and sisters into our hearts, knowing that as we are one, so are we one with their longing, their homelessness, and their displacement from the comfort of their homeland. We too are the lost and the longing. We are the mothers, the fathers, and the children who hold on to hope, hold on to the dream of religious freedom, and to the dream of returning home. We cannot close our eyes or turn our heads away from the truth of the tragedy of Tibet, because so long as it exists, the threat to their very existence threatens us as well. There is no freedom for any one of us until there is freedom for every one of us. We breathe in the heavy dark elements of oppression and we breathe out the promise of freedom. We hold on to the image of a homecoming for each and every Tibetan person. Until their day of freedom, we all remain imprisoned in their condition of exile. May we all be blessed with the freedom to live, and to worship as we choose; may we all be set free.

I once heard someone say that you have to watch the ways in which you live because you might be the only "bible" anyone ever reads. His Holiness, The Dalai Lama, is our living bible, our evidence of a way of being that most of us can only begin to imagine as a possibility while living in this human, ego-laden form. He reminds us, in his words and by his ways, of the importance of being wholly dedicated to the path of enlightenment - by living fully, mindfully, and kindly in each of our moments. The Dalai Lama tells us his religion is kindness and we see no evidence to the contrary. He is a living example of loving kindness and compassion. We see in him, a heart that has no hardness. We see in him, a living example of tolerance and forgiveness. May we all live in a consciousness of loving kindness, even as we are tempted to judge those whose hearts have yet not been opened.

In this time of striving for personal transcendence and global transformation, let us remember to pray for the healing of those who are stuck in the mire of hatred and bigotry. Let us ask that they learn, as we also struggle to learn, by the loving examples of kindness and compassion demonstrated by His Holiness. May we all be set free from the restraints of our own limited thinking, our own egos, our own fears, our own attachments. May we see that the freedom of Tibet will only come as a result of our being willing to give up our own hatreds, our own bigotry. May we each be "a lamp onto ourselves," in order to recognize the fundamental truth of our unity with all beings.

The End. The Beginning

May the blessings of all that is holy, sacred, and divine rest upon you and upon all sentient beings. May the power of love and compassion illuminate your heart and abide in the hearts of all. May all beings live as expressions of loving kindness. May all beings live in peace. Now and forever more.

Amen. Namaste. Om. Shanti. Peace.

Seminars, Lectures and Workshops

Reverend Lori Cardona is available
for education seminars and speaking engagements.
Currently available workshops include:
"Nurturing Your Spirit" and "Spirit At Work".

Other services include: spiritually-focused
psychotherapy, marriages, holy unions, funerals,
memorials, baby blessings/baptisms, prayer
services.

You can contact her via
Interfaith Alliance Ministries.
P.O. Box 531432
Miami Shores, FL. 33153.
(305) 756-6704.
E-mail: IAMinistries@aol.com

Notes

Notes